MW00452167

The Lettering Workbook

FOR SMALL TIP

Brush Pen

A Simple Guide To
Hand Lettering & Modern Calligraphy

RICCA'S GARDEN

ricca_garden

info@riccagarden.com

Published & Designed in Brisbane, Australia

First print: Nov 2022

© Ricca's Garden. All rights reserved. No part of this publication may be reproduced, distributed, or transmitted, in any form or by any means, including photocopying, recording, or other electronic or mechanical methods, without prior written permission of the publisher, except in the case of brief quotations embodied in critical review and certain other non-commercial uses permitted by copyright law.

Hello Friends!

Welcome to *The Lettering Workbook for Small Tip Brush Pens*! This is a follow-up to the previous book, *Lettering Workbook for Absolute Beginners*, where we explored five lettering styles (including monoline, faux calligraphy, brush lettering, serif, and san serif). Since then, there have been many requests to explore more brush lettering styles, so after months of preparation, it's finally here!

In this book, we will be practicing with a small tip brush pen. If you are here for the first time, don't worry! We will start from the beginning with terminology, basic strokes, and three brush lettering styles. We will also be looking at how to create embellishments like wreaths, flourishes, and shadows. So you will not only develop your lettering skills but also learn how to create well-composed designs.

Don't forget to download and print your FREE practice sheets with this workbook. Scan the QR code below or type https://riccagarden.com/lettering-workbook-small-tip/ into your web browser!

NOW, LET'S GET STARTED!

TABLE OF CONTENTS

Getting Started with Brush Lettering

Wherever you are with your lettering practice, it is always useful to explore the different types of tools available and how to use them.

This guide focuses on brush lettering, a type of calligraphy that is done with brush pens. Unlike cursive writing, where words can be written in one stroke without lifting the pen, brush lettering is written with a set of basic strokes. You will be amazed at how quickly and naturally you will improve as you learn these strokes with the help of this guide. In addition, there will also be detailed information on different pens, particularly small tip brush pens, which this workbook is designed for.

ALL ABOUT BRUSH PENS!

BRUSH PENS VS. POINTED PENS

You might often see people doing calligraphy using two main kinds of tools: brush pens and pointed pens, both are great to use and have their own unique look. So, which one should you start with?

Generally, brush pens are recommended for beginners because they are easier to use. Unlike brush pens which already contain pigment, pointed pens may need more time to get used to as their changeable nibs need to be prepped when new (some people burn the tip or stick it into a potato for 15 minutes). You will also need to dip and blot your pointed pen, which can get quite messy when you are not familiar with the tool. All in all, you should still experiment and have fun in your practice, so don't be shy to learn with a pointed pen as well!

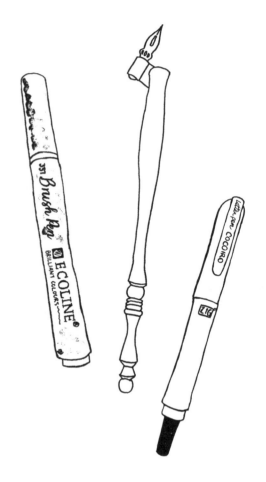

DIFFERENT TYPES OF BRUSH PENS

The 2 main kinds of brush pens are bristle (made with natural or synthetic hair) or felt:

Bristle brush pens: Compared to natural hairbrush pens, synthetic bristles are easier to handle as they have more spring to them. The softness of natural hairbrushes makes them more difficult to control, even though they can hold more ink and they generally last longer than synthetic bristles.

Felt tips: Felt tips are made from one piece of plastic, so they are the easiest to control. They can vary in softness and size, but they all bounce back to their original shape after each stroke. They are one of the most popular types of pens used in calligraphy and are especially recommended for this workbook!

Brush Tip Sizes

All brush pens have different tip sizes, but they are usually put into two categories: small or large. The tip size you choose will determine the scale of your work. The small tip pen is usually suitable for smaller-scale work, and the large tip pen for larger-scale work. The practice pages in this workbook are created particularly for small tip brush pens which are great for beginners! Large tip pens generally take more time to get used to!

Should I get a soft-tip or a hard-tip brush pen?

The brush pen that is ideal for you will depend on how heavy-handed you are. In general, if you are heavy-handed, a firmer-tipped pen may be better; if you are light-hand, softer tips will be suitable. This is because the more pressure you put on the pen (and the angle at which it is held), the wider the line will be.

However, do allow yourself to experiment with different pens to get to know how they feel. Below are some small tip brush pen recommendations, great for beginners and letterers at any level:

Small tip brush pens

Tombow Fudenosuke (Hard Tip)

Ease of control: ★★★★☆

Tip Flexibility：★☆☆☆☆

Tombow Fudenosuke is highly regarded as one of the best pens for beginners because of its sturdy spongy tip. The hard tip may be best for more heavy-handed letterers. The tip is less flexible when pressure is applied, so it makes more precise strokes. Beginners may find it easier to make thin upstrokes with this pen!

Tombow Fudenosuke (Soft Tip)

Ease of control: ★★★☆☆

Tip Flexibility： ★★★☆☆

The softness of the tip means that this pen needs more control. The soft tip can create a wider line when pressure is applied, so letters tend to come out larger than with the hard tip.

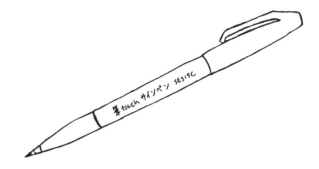

Pentel Fude Touch Pen

Ease of control: ★★★★☆

Tip Flexibility： ★★★☆☆

This pen is another favorite of many and is often compared to the Tombow Fudenosuke pens. In terms of softness, the Pentel Fude Touch pen is somewhere between the Tombow hard and soft tip and is very easy to control. This pen has great durability, and the ink lasts for a long time!

Marvy Uchida Le Pen Flex

Ease of control: ★★★★☆

Tip Flexibility： ★★★☆☆

This Marvy pen is ideal for those looking for a balance between a hard and soft tip. The tip has great bounce, so it is easy to control despite its softness. Make sure you are buying pens that say "Flex" as the barrel design is similar to Marvy's other pens!

Paper

When starting brush lettering, it might be obvious to think about the pens you will use, and perhaps less so about the paper. The paper just as important to bring out the best in your work. Different paper will vary in weight and in the way it absorbs ink. In general, the smoother the paper, the less likely the pen will fray, and the heavier the paper, the less likely your pen will bleed through. This may vary depending on whether your pen has alcohol-based ink (such as Copic or Sharpie), which tends to bleed through the paper more easily. Here are some recommended types of paper, suitable for practicing and final work:

Rhodia Paper

Rhodia is one of the most popular brands among calligraphers and hand letterers as it is pointed pen and brush pen friendly. Rhodia is great for practicing or journalling as it comes in plain, grid, and dot format. The paper is smooth and absorbs ink well without bleeding.

Tracing paper

Tracing paper is perfect to practice with because you can see your guide sheets just by placing them underneath. It will also come in handy when you move on to making compositions because you can use it to trace your designs without having to start all over again. Another advantage is that tracing paper absorbs less ink in the long run, so it is a money saver too! Popular brands include Strathmore and Canson, but most brands are suitable for practice.

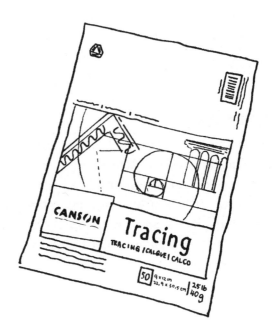

HP 32 PREMIUM PAPER

Another great choice of practice paper that is brilliant white and very affordable. At 120gsm it is a sturdy and smooth copy paper. To add to that, it's a high-quality paper for you to print your free practice sheets that come with this guide — definitely a win-win!

BRISTOL PAPER

This is a smoother, heavier paper (250-270 GSM) which is ideal for final work (heavier paper tends to be more expensive). Its smoothness allows your brush pen to effortlessly glide without catching or fraying. Be sure to choose smooth Bristol paper instead of vellum, which is more textured.

MARKER PAPER

Marker paper is a good alternative to tracing paper. While marker paper is more opaque, it still has enough translucency for you to clearly see your guide sheets underneath. It has a smoother surface than tracing paper, thus more expensive.

WATERCOLOR PAPER

This is perhaps the most textured and heaviest paper (usually around 300gsm). Watercolor paper has a beautiful feel to it, and it works best with watercolor brushes or water brush pens. There are 3 kinds of watercolor paper: hot-pressed, cold-pressed, and rough. Hot-pressed is the most suitable among the three for brush pens as it is the smoothest.

OTHER RECOMMENDED SUPPLIES

While practicing, it is always good to have your basics on hand—pencils, erasers, and rulers (for creating your own guidelines or sketching out your designs). Many hand letterers like to use childhood classics like Crayola markers to practice lettering because their tips can create thick and thin strokes when you hold it at an angle and apply different pressure.

POSITION & POSTURE

Here are some tips on how to position yourself and your materials as comfortably as possible! A general rule to stick to is to sit up straight with your shoulders back. Sit either in the middle of your chair or nearer to the edge and try not to lean on the backrest! Leaning back while you're working and gives you less control of your arm, as well as changes the perspective you have of your paper and thus you work. Ideally, your chair should be at a height where your legs fit comfortably underneath the desk, and where your elbows can just graze the edge.

When it comes to holding your brush pen, hold your pen roughly at a 45-degree angle and about half an inch above the nib. As you write, try rotating your paper, anticlockwise if you are right-handed, and clockwise if you are left-handed, to see if it will make it easier for you to achieve the slant you want in your lettering!

FOR MY LEFTIE FRIENDS!

Please do not think that being left-handed will get in the way of you being a great letterer, it won't! Many left-handed letterers advise you on just adapting the usual guidelines, like how you sit and hold your pen, to what might suit you best. Here are some tips:

- Be patient and let your ink dry before you continue writing.

- Experiment with how to hold your tools to make them comfortable—if you need to frequently change the position of your arm/hand, go for it!

- Same goes for the paper; feel free to to turn your paper as you write.

- Keep a piece of paper/tracing paper under your hand and use the quickest drying brush pen for your paper; that way you will avoid smudging.

TIPS & TRICKS TO HELP YOU ALONG THE WAY

1. The first tip is to breathe, which we might forget to do as we concentrate, but keeping a steady breath as you write will help you relax and allow your writing to become a meditative-like practice.

2. Remember be patient with yourself; that way you will relax more and notice a natural progression.

3. Don't be afraid to make mistakes. They help you see what you can get better at! Observe your mistakes, and maybe even make little notes near your letters to keep track of what you can improve on.

4. Try to slow down and observe the way you feel with the tools and the process of writing to understand what comes naturally and what needs practicing.

5. Practice basic strokes to build muscle memory and consistency. Basic strokes are the basis of all letters so practicing them will help you with improving shaky lines and transitions from thick downstrokes to thin upstrokes.

6. Don't forget to lift your pen while practicing! Remember that your hand lettering is not cursive hand-writing, but a series of individual strokes, which we will find out more about in the next chapter.

TERMINOLOGY

Before we jump into practicing the basic strokes and writing letters, let's take a look at some terminology that defines different parts of a stroke.

BASELINE This is the line that all the letters rest on. This line keeps them in place and keeps the letters from slowly creeping further up or down the paper.

WAISTLINE This is the line where most of the lowercase letters meet at the top (e.g. o, n, a)

ASCENDER LINE This is a higher line, where the tips of taller letters meet (e.g. t, b, l)

DESCENDER LINE A line below the baseline. Some lowercase letters have lines that dip and reach the descender line (g, y, p, q).

X-HEIGHT This is how tall the lowercase letter x is. It is used to refer to the space between the baseline and the waistline.

ASCENDER Any part of a letter that goes above the waistline.

DESCENDER Any part of a letter that extends past the baseline.

CROSS STROKE A horizontal stroke that strikes through letters like t and f.

FLOURISH The pretty decorative swirls that are often added as a fancy embellishment to the letters.

LETTERFORM Basic shape of the letter.

All the terminology may seem incredibly confusing at first but keeping these terms in mind will help to keep your letters consistent and in the right place. Now let us have a look at the basic strokes and drills.

Basic Strokes & Drills

Before we start writing letters, we need to understand the basic strokes they are made of. The basic strokes not only help you create consistency with your letterforms, but they are also a great way to warm up your wrists and serve as a great reminder of the fundamental principles of lettering.

Upstroke

Common Problems

(Shaky lines, lines are too thick)

This is a thin line that starts from the baseline and is drawn upwards. Be sure that your upstroke is NOT a flick—what you're aiming for is a consistently thin line that starts from the baseline and goes up. Also, remember to pace yourself and keep your spacing as equal as you can. Equal spacing is important for the symmetry of your lettering. When you start practicing your upstrokes, do not worry about shaky lines. You will develop control with practice. Enjoy the process and be patient with yourself.

Downstroke

Common Problem

(Inconsistent pressure)

As you may have guessed, the downstroke is the opposite of the upstroke. It is a thick stroke that starts from above and comes down. Again, we're looking for a smooth, and consistent thick line, so apply the same pressure from the top to the bottom.

Underturn

A — W — B — D

A — W — B — D

A — W — B — D

(Too narrow at the bottom, not releasing pressure at the right time)

Once you have practiced your upstrokes and downstrokes, you can combine the two by writing underturns and overturns. You can find this stroke in letters such as a, i, and d. As you can see, the underturn starts at the waistline, comes down (thick downstroke) then curves up (thin upstroke). Write your underturn with one sweeping movement, starting with the increased pressure that lightly releases as you turn up. Start to release as you reach the bottom of your downstroke (about ⅔ down) and let your line get thinner as you curve into your thin upstroke. Avoid the common mistake of releasing your pen too early/late. Practice this until your underturn has consistent thickness and thinness, and until the downstroke and upstroke are parallel, regardless of the slant.

W — B — W — B — W — B

Overturn

A — W — B — D

A — W — B — D

A — W — B — D

(Not enough contrast between thick & thin strokes, the lines are not parallel)

The overturn is the reverse of the underturn. You can find this stroke in letters like m or n. Again, just like the underturn, you want to practice applying different pressure to your pen, rising up lightly with a thin upstroke, curving at the top, and applying more pressure as you lower into a thick downstroke. Always check for equal spacing and keep it parallel with the up and downstrokes!

W — B — W — B — W — B

COMPOUND CURVE

(Curves are too narrow, lines are not parallel, upstrokes are too thick)

As you can see, we are gradually combining strokes to make more complex ones. The compound curve is a combination of your overturn and underturn. Compound curves feature in letters like m, n, and h, and they are used to connect letters. Once again, compound curves are to be written in one movement without lifting the pen. Start from the bottom left of the baseline, rise with a thin upstroke, and curve down into a thick downstroke, then repeat an upstroke. The final result should be two equal curves made from two thin lines and one thick line in the middle. Avoid flicks at the beginning and end of your line.

OVAL

Common Problems

(Applying pressure too late, the oval is not closed, no clear variation in the line weight)

An oval is just an elongated circle written at a slight angle. You see ovals in o, a, and g. The key to making good ovals is starting at the right place so your lines can meet into a seamless shape. The oval is another exercise of changing the pressure of your pen for thick and thin lines. One way to start is with a light upstroke (to the right, at around 1 o'clock), curve anticlockwise and come into a thick downstroke. Curve at the baseline again but this time come into a thin upstroke to meet your starting point. Practice keeping your starting/finishing points at the same thickness. As you practice this basic stroke, try to avoid mistakes such as not closing your oval or applying pressure too late or early.

Ascending Loop

(Applying pressure too late, the loop is too small, no clear variation in the line weight)

You can find ascending loops in letters like h, b, d, and k—all letters that go above the waistline. Start at the waistline and rise with a thin upstroke, curve anticlockwise at the ascender line, and lower into a thick downstroke. The downstroke should join with your starting point at the waistline.

Descending Loop

Common Problems

(Releasing pressure too early, the loop is too small, no clear variation in the line weight)

The descending loop is similar to the ascending loop, only upside down. The descending loop is part of letters such as g and j. The loop of this stroke is always on the left side except for the letter q, in which case the loop is on the right. This time, start from the waistline, lower into a thick downstroke that curves at the descender line. and rises with a thin upstroke into a loop that reaches baseline, the middle of the stem.

ADDITIONAL DRILLS

In addition to practicing the basic strokes, here are some additional drills perfect for all your lettering warm-up needs!

Let's start with the first drill. Make connected upstrokes and downstrokes to help you create consistent thick and thin lines. Start from the baseline and rise with a thin upstroke at a slight angle. Lift your pen at the ascender line. Come down from the same point with a thick downstroke. Essentially, you are making a repeated V shape while trying to maintain line weight and keeping the spacing consistent. Remember to lift your pen after each stroke.

Lift your pen at the dotted line!

This next drill is a series of 3 connected underturns. Begin with a thick downstroke from the waistline and curve into a thin upstroke. Keep the thick and thin lines parallel and be consistent with the slant of the curves.

For practicing overturns, the same principle applies. Try to keep your thick and thin strokes parallel and curve at the same angle!

Now let's try a series of ascending loops. For this drill, start your upstroke from the baseline and connect it to an ascending loop. Instead of finishing the ascending loop at the baseline, release pressure when you are 2/3 down the waistline. Transit the stroke into an underturn. Join the next loop by repeating the process. Here we are trying to keep the size of the loop consistent.

A

W

B

D

A

W

B

D

A

W

B

D

To make a series of joining descending loops, start an upstroke from the baseline to the waistline. Lift your pen and lower it into a downstroke that loops clockwise at the descender line. Lift your pen at the baseline before you start another upstroke, then follow with the next descending loop.

A

W

B

D

A

W

B

D

A

W

B

D

THE ALPHABET

After warming up with the basic strokes, it is finally time to start writing the alphabet. If you need more practice, remember that there are practice sheets available for you to download. You could also practice with a piece of tracing paper overlaying the practice sheet.

As you practice letters, notice how they are each made of the basic strokes we have covered so far. Remind yourself of the fundamentals. Make sure you lift your pen after each stroke, practice thin upstrokes, thick downstrokes, and equally spaced underturns and overturns. Also, remember to keep all of your letters slanted at the same angle. You got this!

LOWERCASE ALPHABET

a

Make an oval that connects to the entrance stroke.

Make an entrance stroke, a thin upstroke from the baseline. Do not go all the way to the waistline, entrance strokes always finish about ⅔ up when you are connecting to an oval.

Join an underturn from the thin side of the oval.

1 + 2 **O** + 3

b

Now add a reverse oval. Normally, we begin the oval on the upper right however, to make a reverse oval, start on the left.

Start with an entrance stroke.

1 + 2 + 3

Add an ascending loop. Lift your pen at the baseline.

4 Finish off with a loop at the baseline and an exit stroke that reaches the waistline.

c

Start a curve, similar to how you would with an oval and curve into downstroke. At the baseline, curve into a thin upstroke and lift your pen when you are almost reaching the waistline.

1 + 2 **C** 3

C's are oval variations, you are essentially leaving your oval open. Make an entrance stroke and lift your pen.

Start with an entrance stroke that goes ⅔ up from base to waistline.

Join an ascending loop to your oval. Finish by curving up into an underturn from the baseline. Lift your pen at the waistline.

Add an oval. Remember to start your oval with light pressure moving upward. Add pressure as you curve down. Release pressure as you curve back to meet your starting point.

Start your oval from ¼ below the waistline to make a small loop. Add pressure as you curve anticlockwise.

Release pressure as you transition from down to upstroke. Lift your pen when you are ¼ away from the waistline.

E is another variation of an oval. Make the entrance stroke.

After your entrance stroke, make an ascending loop that passes the baseline.

Add a final exit stroke.

When you reach ⅔ beneath the baseline, release pressure as you curve anticlockwise at the descender line. Finish your loop at the baseline and lift your pen.

Lowercase Alphabet

Draw an entrance stroke and finish about ⅔ up from the baseline.

Add an exit stroke.

Make an oval, then add a descending loop. Always check the interior spacing of your ovals and loops. Try to keep them consistent.

Add an ascending loop that finishes at the baseline.

From the baseline, add a compound curve.

Make an entrance stroke.

Finish your i with a dot just above the thick stem.

I may be the easiest letter to learn. Make an entrance stroke.

Add an underturn.

j

Make an entrance stroke.   Add a descending loop.   Finish off with a dot on the descending loop.

j + j + j + j

Add a final upstroke from the baseline as an exit stroke.

k

After your entrance stroke, add an ascending loop.   On the right side of the ascending loop, make a small loop.

k + l + k

Add an underturn and finish just below the waistline.

l

After your entrance stroke, attach an ascending loop. Transition to an underturn when you pass the waistline.

l + l

LOWERCASE ALPHABET

A

W
m   *n* + *n* + *n*

B
Make an overturn. Lift your pen at the baseline.

Finish with a compound curve, lift pen at the waistline. Remember to keep the strokes parallel and evenly spaced.

Add another overturn that connects to the first one.

D

A

W

B

D

A

W

B

D

A

W
n   *n* + *n*

B
Once you get used to the letter m, n is very easy. N is similar to m, only you make one overturn, then a compound curve.

D

A

W

B

D

A

W

B

D

A

W
o   *)* + *O* + *o*

B
Create an oval.

Make an entrance stroke.

To finish, add a small curved horizontal line at the top of your oval. This horizontal line functions to connect to the next letter – You will learn more about this in later chapters.

D

A

W

B

D

A

W

B

D

On the right side of the descending loop, ¼ beneath the waistline, curve clockwise into a reverse oval.

Make an entrance stroke.

Add a descending loop.

Instead of finishing your oval, make a small loop at the baseline and strike through the oval with an exit stroke.

Add a descending loop. This time, the descending loop will face the right.

Add an upstroke from base to waistline.

Make an entrance stroke and add an oval.

Make an entrance stroke from base to waistline.

Make a small loop going anticlockwise just above the waistline.

Transition to an underturn.

LOWERCASE ALPHABET

S is a unique letter that requires you to draw a variation of the basic stroke. Make an entrance stroke.

Make a small loop on the waistline and curve anticlockwise. Make an S shape with a downstroke. Curve clockwise at baseline and strike through the S with an exit stroke.

Make an entrance stroke.

Finish with a cross stroke.

Add a downstroke, then release pressure ⅔ below the waistline as you transition to an underturn.

Make an upstroke.

Add 2 underturns. Lift pen at the waistline each time.

Make a compound curve. As you finish your final upstroke, loop at the waistline. The final loop is the stroke that connects to the following letter.

Add an underturn, and lift your pen at the waistline.

Make an entrance stroke.

Add your second underturn and make a loop at the waistline. This final stroke should have very little pressure. Practice keeping a smooth, consistent line. Don't worry if your hand is shaky at first.

Strike through the middle downstroke with a thin diagonal upstroke that slightly curves at the ends.

Make a compound curve. Practice keeping the up and downstroke parallel.

LOWERCASE ALPHABET

A

W $\mathcal{Y}$

B

D

Add a descending loop.

1 $\mathcal{V}$ 2   + $\mathcal{Y}$ 3   +   5 $\mathcal{Y}$

Make a compound curve.   4

Add an exit stroke from where the loop finishes.

A

W

B $\mathcal{Y}$ $\mathcal{Y}$ $\mathcal{Y}$ $\mathcal{Y}$ $\mathcal{Y}$ $\mathcal{Y}$ $\mathcal{Y}$

D

A

W

B $\mathcal{Y}$

D

A

Make an overturn.

W $\mathcal{Z}$

B   1 $\mathcal{V}$ + $\mathcal{Z}$ 2   +   4 $\mathcal{Z}$

D   3

Strike through the upper part of the oval with an upstroke.

At the bottom of your overturn, start a reverse oval, making a thicker downstroke as you graze the descender line and curve back up.

A

W

B $\mathcal{Z}$ $\mathcal{Z}$ $\mathcal{Z}$ $\mathcal{Z}$ $\mathcal{Z}$ $\mathcal{Z}$ $\mathcal{Z}$

D

A

W

B $\mathcal{Z}$

D

A

W

B

D

A

W

B

D

A

W

B

D

Add another downstroke and transition to an underturn at the baseline. Finish at the waistline.

Draw a slanted downstroke from the ascender line. Add pressure until you reach 2/3 down the waistline and release pressure as you curve back up clockwise. Strike through the middle of the downstroke.

Make a small entrance stroke just below the ascender line.

Add a downstroke & release pressure towards the baseline. Transition to reverse underturn.

To the right side, make a reverse oval

Add a curve that starts thin and thickens into a downstroke. Make a loop at the baseline.

Like the lowercase C, the uppercase is also a variation of an oval. Start upstroke from just below the waistline,

Loop anticlockwise at the ascender line.

Add pressure as you curve down and release pressure about 2/3 down from the waistline.

Curve up with light pressure from the baseline.

Uppercase Alphabet

A

W

B

First, make an entrance stroke.   +   Add a downstroke and transit to reverse underturn towards the baseline.   +

Add an upstroke from waist to ascender line, curve into downstroke.

At the baseline, make a loop w. light pressure and leave a tail outside the D.

D

D uses a large reverse oval, so again you will be practicing the steady transition from upstroke to downstroke.

A

W

B

D

A

W

B

D

A

W

B

Make an upstroke from below waistline and loop anticlockwise at the ascender line. Release pressure as you end your curve at the waistline.   +

Start your next curve thin and add pressure into your downstroke. Release pressure as you curve upward from the baseline.

D

A

W

B

D

A

W

B

D

A

W

B

Start a downstroke just below the ascender line. Curve clockwise, transition into a reverse underturn.   +   Add a cross stroke at the ascender line and another smaller cross ¼ above the waistline.   +

D

A

W

B

D

A

W

B

D

A
W
B
D

Start with an uppercase C shape.

Add another descending loop and loop through the stem.

+

A
W
B
D

A
W
B
D

Make a small entrance stroke.

Finish with a crossbar that starts/finishes outside the downstrokes.

+

+

Add a downstroke and transit into a reverse underturn at the baseline.

Leave a small space and make another downstroke parallel to the first one. Transition into an underturn at the baseline.

A
W
B
D

A
W
B
D

Make a downstroke and release pressure ⅔ below the waistline. Curve into a reverse underturn at the baseline.

+

Make a small entrance stroke beneath the ascender line and lift your pen.

A
W
B
D

A
W
B
D

J — Draw a downstroke and finish with a reverse underturn from the baseline.

Join with a curved cross bar.

K — Make a small entrance stroke beneath the ascender line.

Add a downstroke and finish with a reverse underturn.

To make the arm and leg of the K, on the right side, add one upstroke from the waist to ascender line, then one downstroke from waist to baseline.

L — Capital L's are done in one stroke. Start with an entrance stroke just below the waistline. Continue by drawing an ascending loop. Make sure you add pressure into your downstroke!

Release pressure as you make a small loop at the baseline and finish with a thinner horizontal line.

Start with a small entrance stroke.

Add a downstroke that curves into a reverse underturn from the baseline. Lift your pen just above the waistline.

Add an overturn. Add a compound curve

Make a small entrance stroke below the ascender line.

Add a downstroke that curves into a reverse underturn from the baseline.

Add a compound curve starting from the middle of your downstroke.

Bring an upstroke starting just below the waistline.

Loop anticlockwise below the ascender line and come into a downstroke.

Finish the oval with an upstroke and lift your pen before touching the top loop.

Uppercase Alphabet

P

Start with a small entrance stroke beneath the ascender line.

Add a downstroke and transit into a reverse underturn, and finish just above the waistline.

Start a reverse oval from the middle of the stem. Release pressure as you meet the stem below the waistline to finish.

Q

Repeat the capital O shape.

Finish your Q with a small horizontal line through the bottom of the O shape and leave a tail.

R

Make a small entrance stroke.

Make a downstroke, curve into a reverse underturn and lift your pen just above the waistline.

Start a reverse oval from the middle of the stem and lift your pen when it meets the lower part of the stem.

Finish with a short downstroke from the end of the loop.

Make a horizontal line between waist and ascender line.

Loop at the ascender line and lower into a downstroke. Curve clockwise into an upstroke at the baseline and lift your pen just above the waistline.

Add a cross bar on top of your downstroke.

T has the same letterform as F, but this time with one crossbar. Start a downstroke just below the ascender line and curve into a reverse underturn from the baseline.

Make a small entrance stroke.

+

Add an underturn. Start your downstroke from the ascender line to the baseline. Curve into a parallel upstroke and lift your pen at the ascender line.

+

Add another downstroke, curve back up into an underturn, and lift your pen just before the waistline.

UPPERCASE ALPHABET

Make an entrance stroke.   +

If you prefer, you can draw a pointier V by lifting your pen at the end of your downstroke and add a slanted upstroke.

Add an underturn. Start with a downstroke and finish with an upstroke just above the ascender line.

Make an entrance stroke.   +

Add an underturn and lift your pen ¼ below the ascender line.

+   Add another underturn and finish your upstroke at the ascender line.

Make a small entrance stroke.   +

Add an underturn starting from the ascender line but lift your pen just below the waistline.

+   Strike through the stem with a slanted upstroke starting from the baseline to the ascender line.

Make an entrance stroke. + Add an underturn. + Add a descending loop and finish with an upstroke through the stem.

The Z shape is mainly done in one stroke. Just be patient with yourself as you practice transitioning between thin and thick strokes.

+ Add a small horizontal line in the middle of the stem.

Make a horizontal line at the ascender then loop anticlockwise. Continue down with full pressure and once you reach the baseline, loop clockwise then finish with another horizontal line.

PRACTICE NUMBERS TOO!

CONNECTING LETTERS

Now that we have covered writing individual letters, it is time to move on to connecting them together. The best advice is to keep the length and spacing of your connection consistent. Keep in mind what letters you are going to write next so you know how long your connecting stroke should be. You will find that it is often a game of taking away the entrance or exit strokes of letters like the ones you see below:

As you write, you will notice how some letters naturally flow into each other, whereas others might not. When that happens, don't worry! There is often more than one way to connect letters and you will naturally find your favorite connection as you practice.

DIFFERENT WAYS TO CONNECT O & U:

DIFFERENT WAYS TO CONNECT W & I:

The reverse compound curve can be used when you are connecting your underturn to an overturn.

——— This stroke is done without lifting the pen. ———

Finally, you might feel relieved to know that you do not have to connect every single letter. Especially when you are writing your first letter in capital.

On the next few pages, you will find a great series of words to practice for connecting. It might be a good idea to get a different colored pen and mark the kind of transitions you see.

Connecting Letters

be be be

ac ac ac

in in in

un un un

ou ou ou

ob ob ob

pu pu pu

ld ld ld

th   *t tt th*

Try connecting the cross stroke of
the t to the ascending loop of h.

tu   *tu tu*

ss   *ss ss*

rr   *rr rr*

gh   *gh gh*

gl   *gl gl*

mb   *mb mb*

mf   *mf mf*

Connecting Letters

art   *art*

kind   *kind*

life   *life*

dear   *dear*

help   *help*

time   *time*

feel   *feel*

hope   *hope*

baby *baby*

beach *beach*

think *think*

future *future*

perfect *perfect*

fortune *fortune*

simple *simple*

forever *forever*

Finding Your Own Style

Once you have practiced the basic strokes and alphabet, it is time to find your own personal style in lettering. The basic rules are important to help us get started, however, like all art practices, brush lettering is personal, so it is great to be able to express your very own unique touch through your work. Even though you could have been following examples and tracing over practice sheets, there might be certain ways you would prefer writing your letters. Do not be afraid to create flaris or styles that you find interesting, even if you might not see them anywhere else.

In your personal practice, it is nice to make your environment as comfortable and the experience as enjoyable as possible, you could put on some music or even practice lettering at your favorite place, just to help you tap into yourself. Of course, we would to improve our lettering skills, but that can also happen while we enjoy the process and remind ourselves that lettering is also a relaxing, meditative self-care practice.

Playing with the letterform

Try to create a different look for your letters by playing with the letterform. Firstly, let's try exaggerating the loops.

Next, try to stretch the letters—make the entrance and exit strokes longer and leave more space in between.

BOUNCE LETTERING

When practicing the basic brush lettering style, our letters have stayed within the guidelines so far. If you are looking to try a more playful and whimsical kind of lettering, try bounce lettering.

Look at the example above where the letters have raised above the waistline or dipped below the baseline, creating a "bouncing" look.

Notice in the example how the letterform of "m" is loosened, with the height of the first and second curve being different. Changing the height of the curve within the same letter also helps to add bounce to your letters. You can try changing the height of the curves in "w" too.

When you are just starting out, bounce lettering can be hard to master, and you might think your letters look messy and unbalanced. If that happens, try to keep your letters' x-height similar. When you break through the waist or baseline, keep the bounce on the same level (like the letters h and m you see in the example). Not all letters need to break through the guidelines to achieve the bouncy look.

There is no exact formula to achieve bounce lettering, so allow yourself to experiment with different ways to write your letters.

Flourishing

We have all seen book covers, shop signs, and titles that start and finish with swirls that seem so effortless and proportionate. This is called flourishing. Flourishing is a great way to practice shapes and swirls that accentuate and decorate our letters.

However intimidating flourishing may seem, try to see it as a way to relax into your pen strokes. Keep your hand light as you flourish and avoid anchoring onto the page. Be patient with yourself and let the flourishing strokes flow. The proportions and your pen control will improve naturally with practice over time.

While flourishing is a great way to create more symmetry in your lettering, the main thing to remember is to make sure your words are still readable. Make sure your flourishes are not easily mistaken as a letter like below:

This looks like an "e" so try to avoid it.

Flourishing is based on the principle of ovals, so see if you can spot the big and small ovals in them.

Next, let's look at the ideal spots to add flourishes.

Ascending loops

You can add this kind of flourish to letters such as b, d, f, h, k, and l.

Descending Loops

This next set of flourishes is perfect to add to letters like g, y, p, y, and z.

The End of a Word

Flourishes at the end of a word extend from the exit stroke.

Underneath a Word

Flourishes made underneath a word are usually extended from the downstroke. Sometimes, the place for adding this type of flourish is less obvious However, they are great for filling up empty spaces, even though your letter may be in the middle of the word.

Cross Bars

Cross bar flourishes are mainly used in the letter t.

After looking over the examples above, it is time to play and flow!
Let your arm and pen guide you into loops and swirls.

FLOURISHING

Use a pencil or pen to draw the flourish without adding line weight first. As you become more comfortable, start creating line variations with a brush pen.

Focus on transitioning the line weight between downstroke and upstroke.

Flourishing

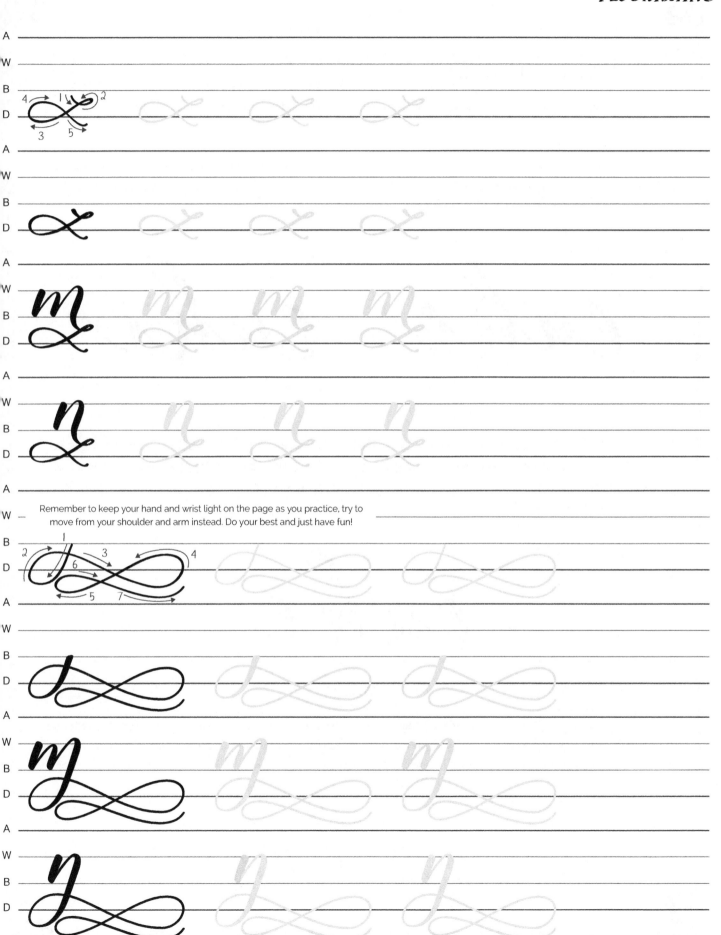

Remember to keep your hand and wrist light on the page as you practice, try to move from your shoulder and arm instead. Do your best and just have fun!

Embellishing your letters

Another way to add character to your lettering is to add shadows, highlights, and outlines!

Shadows

If you want to add shadows, first decide on where the light is shining. The general rule is that the shadow will be on the opposite side of wherever the light is coming from. You can even try this by shining a light on a small object from different angles.

You can see that if the light comes from the top left, the shadows fall on the bottom right and vice versa. Another good trick to learn shadows is by tracing over your lettering with a piece of tracing paper. When you finish tracing, move the paper aside slightly then the overlapping letters can help you gain a better understanding of where your shadows should be.

Try adding shadows with lines too.

Outlines

Try outlining your lettering with a fineliner. Ideally use black or any other dark color that suits the lettering color to make it pop. Remember that you do not have to outline the cross in the intersection. If there is a space between your letter and the outline, do remember to fill in the gap.

Highlights

Another fun way to style your letters is by adding highlights! The easiest way to do so is by adding lines to your letters using a white gel pen. As opposed to adding shadows, this creates the effect that your lettering is rising from the foreground.

Don't have a brush pen with you? Try faux calligraphy!

If you don't have a brush pen on hand or want to letter on surfaces other than paper, try faux calligraphy! Faux calligraphy mimics the look of brush lettering by using the same principle that we have learned so far – keeping the upstroke thin and the downstroke thick!

Start with writing your word in cursive, then thicken the downstrokes by drawing another line next to them. You can leave the blank space between the lines open or fill it in. To be even more creative, you could try drawing different patterns in that space!

You should leave a little space for the downstroke if you do not plan to fill in the gaps.

1. *cake*

2. *cake*

3. *cake*

Exploring more brush lettering styles

There are many ways to write the same alphabet even though we are just brush lettering. The mood and feel of the design can change significantly just by altering the lettering styles. Once we have learned the basics, why don't we try writing our letters differently? Even for a beginner, it is fun to explore the possibilities! Don't worry about getting it right straight away.

Begonia

Begonia is a loopy lettering style. As you can see below, many letters start with a small loop and transit into thick downstrokes. Practice changing the pressure you apply to the brush pen to get a clear variation in the line weight. This fun and theatrical style is perfect for use in party invitations, birthday cards, or lighthearted quotes to frame in your home.

Aa Bb Cc Dd

Ee Ff Gg Hh

Ii Jj Kk Ll

Mm Nn Oo Pp

Qq Rr Ss Tt

Uu Vv Ww Xx

Yy Zz

BEGONIA

Aa

Bb

Cc

Dd

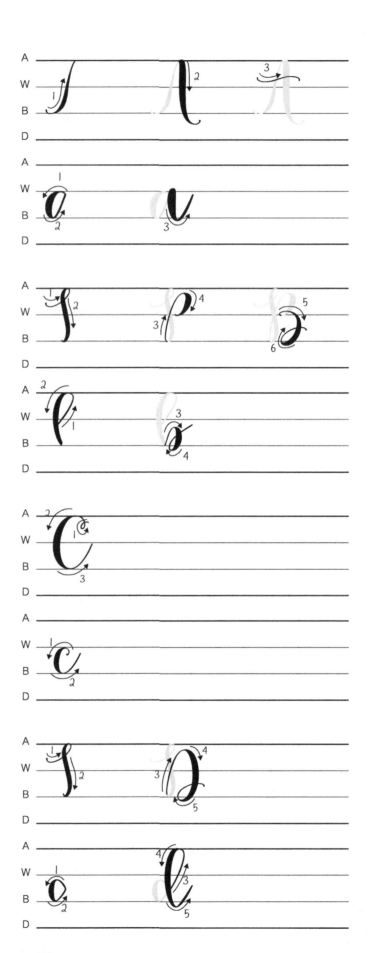

Aa Aa Aa Aa Aa

Aa

Bb Bb Bb Bb Bb

Bb

Cc Cc Cc Cc Cc

Cc

Dd Dd Dd Dd Dd

Dd

Ee

Ff

Gg

Hh

Ee Ee Ee Ee Ee

Ee

Ff Ff Ff Ff Ff

Ff

Gg Gg Gg Gg Gg

Gg

Hh Hh Hh Hh Hh

Hh

BEGONIA

Ii Ii Ii Ii Ii

Ii

Jj Jj Jj Jj Jj

Jj

Kk Kk Kk Kk Kk

Kk

Ll Ll Ll Ll Ll

Ll

BEGONIA

Mm Mm Mm Mm Mm

Mm

Nn Nn Nn Nn Nn

Nn

Oo Oo Oo Oo Oo

Oo

Pp Pp Pp Pp Pp

Pp

BEGONIA

Q q

R r

S s

T t

Qq *Qq* *Qq* *Qq* *Qq*

Qq

Rr *Rr* *Rr* *Rr* *Rr*

Rr

Ss *Ss* *Ss* *Ss* *Ss*

Ss

Tt *Tt* *Tt* *Tt* *Tt*

Tt

BEGONIA

Uu

Vv

Ww

Xx

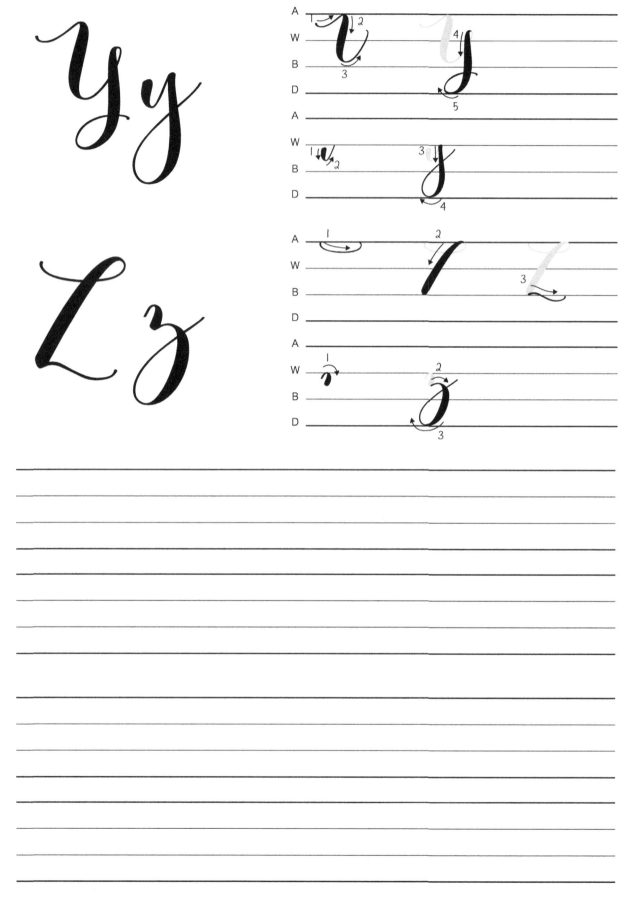

Yy Yy Yy Yy Yy

Yy

Zz Zz Zz Zz Zz

Zz

PRACTICE NUMBERS TOO!

1234567890

Wisteria

This next lettering style, Wisteria, is a chance for you to flex your flourishing muscles. Being more dramatic and elegant, Wisteria will suit wedding invitations and greeting cards if you wish to set a more formal tone. Don't be discouraged to see all the big curves and loops in this style of lettering. You can always grab a pencil to practice drawing the shape of the letters first before worrying about applying pressure with a brush pen. Remember that you can print out additional practice sheets online. You've got this!

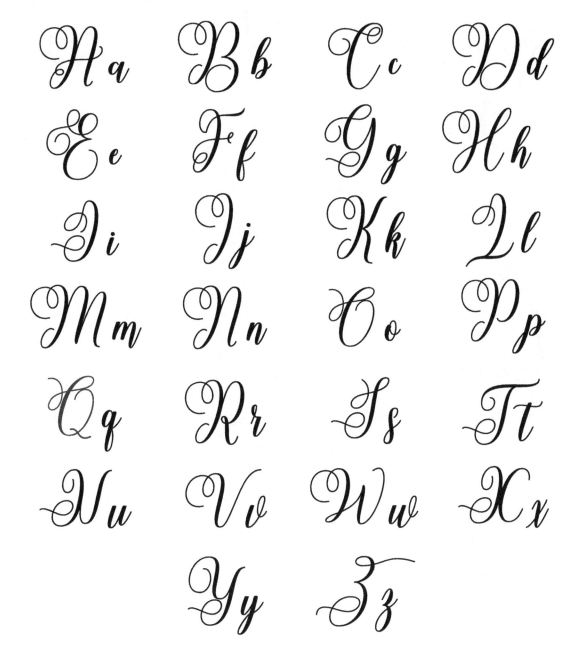

Aa   Aa   Aa   Aa   Aa

Aa

Bb   Bb   Bb   Bb   Bb

Bb

Cc   Cc   Cc   Cc   Cc

Cc

Dd   Dd   Dd   Dd   Dd

Dd

Ee

Ff

Gg

Hh

Ee   Ee   Ee   Ee   Ee

Ee

Ff   Ff   Ff   Ff   Ff

Ff

Gg   Gg   Gg   Gg   Gg

Gg

Hh   Hh   Hh   Hh   Hh

Hh

Ii Ii Ii Ii Ii

Ii

Jj Jj Jj Jj Jj

Jj

Kk Kk Kk Kk Kk

Kk

Ll Ll Ll Ll Ll

Ll

Mm *Mm* *Mm* *Mm* *Mm*

Mm

Nn *Nn* *Nn* *Nn* *Nn*

Nn

Oo *Oo* *Oo* *Oo* *Oo*

Oo

Pp *Pp* *Pp* *Pp* *Pp*

Pp

Qq Qq Qq Qq Qq

Qq

Rr Rr Rr Rr Rr

Rr

Ss Ss Ss Ss Ss

Ss

Tt Tt Tt Tt Tt

Tt

$\mathcal{N}u$

$\mathcal{V}v$

$\mathcal{W}w$

$\mathcal{X}x$

Uu Uu Uu Uu Uu

Uu

Vv Vv Vv Vv Vv

Vv

Ww Ww Ww Ww Ww

Ww

Xx Xx Xx Xx Xx

Xx

Yy *Yy* *Yy* *Yy* *Yy*

Yy

Zz *Zz* *Zz* *Zz* *Zz*

Zz

PRACTICE NUMBERS TOO!

$1\ 2\ 3\ 4\ 5\ 6\ 7\ 8\ 9\ 0$

COMPOSITION

When creating lettering designs, whether it is for a greeting card, invitation, sign, or wall decoration, you need to create a composition. Composition is about the lettering and decorative elements working together in harmony and it is something that many people find difficult. However daunting composition may seem, it is best to just dive in. Start sketching ideas down even though it is not perfect on the first go. As you refine your design, the layout will slowly come together. There's no exact rule on how to compose your design but in this chapter, we will go through some tips on how you can get started.

COMBINING YOUR LETTERING WITH SERIF & SANS SERIF

If you are wondering what serif and sans serif are, they are actually two common typefaces that you might see very often in your daily life. Serif letters are all edged with small decorative strokes like the one you see in Times New Roman font. Usually, it is seen as more formal and elegant. (Please refer to The Lettering Workbook for Absolute Beginners for a full tutorial on the serif style!)

Sans serif on the other hand does not have these small strokes and carries a more modern and informal look. Fonts like Arial or Calibri are sans serif style.

ABCDEFG   ABCDEFG
HIJKLMN   HIJKLMN
OPQRSTU   OPQRSTU
VWXYZ   VWXYZ

SERIF   SANS SERIF

Depending on the mood of your design, you can choose to combine your brush lettering style with either serif or sans serif to help convey the message of your text.

DRAWING A WREATH

Wreaths are a beautiful way to highlight your lettering. Curling leaves and flowers compliment the curls we see in the brush lettering we have covered so far. So, let's try it!

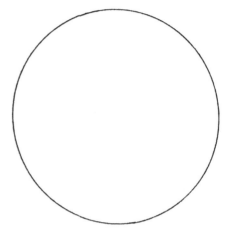

1. Use a pencil to create a guide for your wreath. To create a circle, you can use a stencil, protractor, or anything circular that you can trace around, even a cup.

2. Draw 4 lines to divide the circle into 8 segments, one horizontal, one vertical, and 2 diagonals. Each segment does not have to be exactly even, but it will help you create a more balanced-looking design.

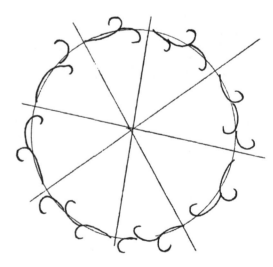

3. Now use a fineliner to create the stems of your wreath. In the example, each segment sticks to 2 or 3 stems. Again, experimentation is always welcomed, but it is also good to keep it simple when you are first starting out.

4. Now that your stems are done, add a simple flower to the end of each stem.

5. Add leaves along the stems.

6. Once your ink has dried, erase the pencil lines, and there you have it, your floral wreath.

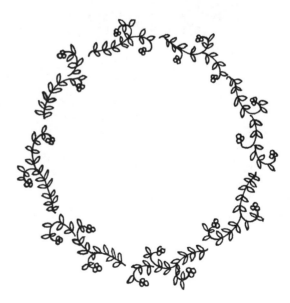

Play around with drawing wreaths using the same method. You can also try leaving the wreath open like the examples below.

CREATE A SIMPLE LAYOUT BY FINDING NEGATIVE SPACE

Now, let's try to use the example quote "You light up my life" to create a simple lettering layout.

1.   Start by writing out the quote in different ways with a pencil. The lettering does not have to be perfect for now, we are just experimenting with the placement of words. This will help you understand spacing and avoid ascenders and descenders bumping into each other. Writing the quote out in different ways will also help you notice when lines are too long/short like the first and second examples. That way you can keep all the lines proportionate to each other.

① *You light up my life*

② *You light up my life*

③ *You light up my life*

2.   The last example seems to be most proportionate, so let's rewrite it properly in about the same size you would want your finished artwork to be. Look for negative spaces in between your letters and circle them if necessary.

You light up my life

3. To improve the layout, you can now extend your letters or add flourishes in the negative spaces you see. You should still be using a pencil at this stage so you can keep making changes until you have found the perfect design.

3. Now you are ready to ink out your design with a brush pen. Erase any pencil marks afterward. Alternatively, you can use tracing paper to trace over your design.

A Week of Appreciation

"A Week of Appreciation" is a 7-day challenge that combines all the things we have learned so far! Just like any artistic craft, developing your hand lettering needs lots of play and practice. Sometimes it can be difficult to stick to a routine and come up with your own ideas, so be sure to make use of any weekly or monthly challenges that inspire you and help with your practice.

In this challenge, we will be writing seven quotes of appreciation. See it as an act of meditative self-care. As you write, think of the meaning of the quotes, remember special people in your life, and thank yourself for setting aside time to do something you love.

Even if this is a 7-day challenge, feel free to adapt it to your needs. If you can't finish a design in one day, don't worry, just pick it up the next day. Using challenges is a way to build skill and consistency. It can take time, but the main thing is to enjoy it.

Day 1: You bring out the joy!

In this first quote, watch the way each letter connects and how the lines are spaced. When you are practicing the quote freehand, try to keep the slant of your letters consistent.

Trace here first.

You have a special way of bringing out the joy in everyone!

Now try it yourself.

DAY 2: I AM SO LUCKY TO KNOW YOU

On day 2, let's try to stretch out the letters. Do it slowly & remember to extend the exit stroke of each letter.

Practice stretching the letters first.

lucky

Now try stretching freehand.

Now complete the quote.

I AM SO

lucky

TO KNOW YOU

Practice again here.

Day 3: Your thoughtfulness is a gift

Today, let's try to play around with the descending loops in the quote by extending them!

Practice here first.

Your thoughtfulness is a gift

You can pause at the intersection of the loop first before extending the stroke.

Make sure there is enough space here so the rest of the quote can fit on top.

Try again here.

Your thoughtfulness is a gift

Now try it yourself.

Day 4: Thank you for being you

Use a fineliner to add shadow lines to your next quote. Imagine the light shining from the left, you can see the lines fall to the right side. Take note of how the final stroke of (y)ou is extended. Draw a parallel line beneath it first before writing the last part of the quote (for being you)!

Trace it here.

Now try it yourself! You can use a pencil to draw some guidelines to help you.

DAY 5: YOU MAKE ME GIGGLE!

On day 5 we get to try out wreaths! Just like we did in the previous chapter, you can use a pencil to divide the circle into eight to help you create a balanced-looking wreath. Do feel free to expand your creativity and change up the design!

Try extending the entrance and exit strokes of 'always' and 'giggle'.

THANK YOU FOR
always
MAKING ME
giggle

When you write your quote, use the curved line as a guide to write "Thank you for".

Now try it yourself! Don't forget to draw your guideline using a pencil first.

Day 6: You give me strength

It is day 6 and before we finish the challenge, let's practice flourishing. You can use a pencil to practice drawing the final flourish at the bottom first. When you are feeling confident after your practice, add line weight to the flourish with a brush pen.

Trace it here.

You give me strength I did not know I had

Practice again here!

Day 7: Do small things with great love

The final quote of this challenge is a great reminder by Mother Teresa. This is a longer quote, so it might be tempting for us to write at the same speed as our usual handwriting. Remember to slow down and lift your pen between each stroke. Finish off the exit stroke with a heart.

Trace here first.

We cannot do great things on this earth, only small things with great love♡

MOTHER TERESA

Now try it yourself!

FOR MAKING IT THIS FAR!

You can always create challenges for yourself like this one.
For example, try designing a quote from your favorite song lyrics, movie, or
poetry for a week, whatever is best for you.

I hope you have enjoyed the practice, and that you enjoy the rest of your brush
lettering journey!

Made in the USA
Las Vegas, NV
23 November 2022

60197249R00059